ADOPTION
AND FOSTERING

A Parent's Guide

Need – 2 – Know

Holly Noseda

First published in Great Britain in 2008 by
Need2Know
Remus House
Coltsfoot Drive
Peterborough
PE2 9JX
Telephone 01733 898103
Fax 01733 313524
www.need2knowbooks.co.uk

Need2Know is an imprint of Forward Press Ltd.
www.forwardpress.co.uk

Contents

Introduction

Whoever you are, whatever your background, the chances are that someone in your life has been affected by adoption.

According to the Post Adoption Centre, one in four people in the UK knows someone with a link to the adoption process. You may not know it and, in some extreme cases, they may not either.

Adoption is everywhere, adoptees and adopters are everywhere, and yet there is so much confusion and outdated information surrounding the process. Dipping your toe in the water can be terrifying and confusing. Trying to explain the process and the journey to your friends, family and colleagues can be even harder!

Adopting and fostering children is an enriching, amazing, challenging, nerve-wracking and wonderful journey and we aim to help shine the light on every step of the process.

Adoption and Fostering – A Parent's Guide has been compiled for anyone considering adoption, embarking on the adoptive journey or wanting to support and understand the experiences of friends or family who are in the process of becoming an adoptive family. The guide also covers fostering; looking at who can foster and how to become a foster carer.

Although the book refers to children as 'your child', it is also an essential guide for all those working with adopted and fostered children, friends and relatives or adopters, foster carers and potential adopters. We will frequently refer to your child but this encompasses sibling groups too.

The majority of the content in this book applies to either the UK as a whole, or England, Scotland and Wales separately. Where possible, information on Northern Ireland is also included.

Adoption is a huge and emotive topic. This book aims to guide you through the initial considerations, making sense of the legislative maze and helping you plan for your new family – emotionally and practically.

What is adoption?

Adoption and Fostering – A Parent's Guide will explain the differences between fostering and adoption; between modern and historic adoption and the differences between babies who have been given up and children who have been removed from birth families by social services teams.

We will talk about the professionals that you will meet along your journey and the application and study that you will be asked to complete before you are approved to adopt your child.

Some statistics to chew over

According to the British Association for Adoption and Fostering, there are around 60,000 children within the care system in England alone. Every year, over 5,000 of these children will become adoptees, with their own stories, family histories and unique medical or psychological needs.

And every year, adopters from all backgrounds are approved and matched with these children to form forever families.

Who can adopt?

The rules on who can adopt are now far broader and fairer than even ten years ago. Same-sex couples, co-habiting couples and single people – historically overlooked – are now legally afforded the same consideration as married couples.

Race, religion and sexuality are no barrier, and the world of adoption is one of rich diversity. There are some restrictions however, and we will look at these in more detail later in the chapters.

We will look at the process, at times frustrating, but peppered with exciting milestones. We will help you to examine your expectations of adoption and prepare yourself and your support network for the early days with your adoptive family.

It is important to understand your own reasons for wanting to adopt, to be able to articulate these and recognise and manage your own hopes and expectations.

Why are children adopted?

To give you a better grasp of the child you may be matched with, we will look at the current situation, the reasons children enter the care system and are eventually adopted and how today's reality differs from the dramatised or historical views of adoption that many of us have grown up with.

We will look at the medical and emotional needs that you may need to cater for and the age groups of children available to adopt.

The process

We will talk you through every step:

- Making your first enquiry with a Local Authority (LA) or adoption agency.
- Preparation groups.
- Home study with a social worker.
- Assessment.
- Official approval.
- Matching with a child.
- Bringing your new family home.
- Post-adoption support.

At the end of every chapter you will find summary information and steps for what to do next. Further along, we provide checklists for everything that you may need to buy and arrange in preparation for your new family.

The adoptive process is gruelling, emotionally exhausting and, at times, frustrating. But it is also one of enlightenment, joy and discovery. Adoption, at its best, brings people together and helps to create loving, happy families.

Chapter One

History of Adoption

Early adoption

Although we now have rules and laws for the way adoption is carried out, the concept of children being raised by maternal and paternal figures that did not biologically 'create' them is nothing new, in fact, it's as old as the hills.

The story of Moses – among others – introduces the idea of adoption in the Bible, and it is believed that a formal system of adoption existed in ancient Arabia.

Over the last century, the laws and guidelines that control adoption in the UK have been through various changes, many of which have been frustratingly slow to roll around. Before 2002, the last major amendment to the 1958 Children Act was 27 years ago, in 1975.

Adoption of babies in the 1960s

For many people unfamiliar with today's reality, the idea of young mums having their illegitimate offspring taken from them under pressure is still likely to spring to mind when you mention adoption. But this stark image bears little relation to the care system of Britain today.

In the 1960s, unmarried mothers felt enormous social pressure to relinquish their children. Now, single parent families are nothing out of the ordinary and many couples are choosing not to get married at all. The landscape is totally different and the reasons behind adoption are far more diverse than ever before.

Sadly, many terrible mistakes were made with babies and birth mothers in the 1960s and 1970s, but lessons have been learnt through these and we – as a society and professionals – are still learning how best to help adoptees and their families to adapt to their new lives.

Relinquished babies and foundlings

Babies 'given up' by birth mothers and made available for adoption are known as 'relinquished babies'. Foundlings, though similar, are far rarer. Foundlings are abandoned children and babies who remain unclaimed by birth mothers and families.

Cases of foundlings are incredibly rare but do still occur from time to time. You may have heard the stories about newborn babies found in hospital car parks or public parks. Often the birth mums are traced and helped to parent their children, but when this is not possible, the babies enter the care system and may eventually be adopted.

Since 1977, as part of The Children Act 1975, abandoned babies in England and Wales have been registered on the Abandoned Children's Register. This happens six months to a year after police begin their enquiries into the birth family of the child.

Babies found before 1977 were simply registered at the Register Office near where they were found and birth certificates contained only what was known of the child, plus a name and surname that had been decided by professionals who had cared for the baby.

As you can imagine, this caused immense confusion and desolation to many foundlings.

'A 2007 study carried out for the British Association for Adoption and Fostering (BAAF) found that 41% of people believed that mothers put up their children for adoption at birth.'

Social services removal

Sadly, the majority of babies and children who are freed for adoption now have entered the care system after being removed from their birth families by social services. We'll explore the reasons further within this book.

Do social workers take children to give to adopters?

Despite what many 'pub experts' like to suggest, the decision to remove children from birth families is never taken lightly and will come after efforts to keep the children supported and safe at home.

There have been controversial newspaper articles about adoption targets and you may well run into these arguments from people outside the adoption world as you continue on your journey.

Please be assured that there are no targets to get children into the already overloaded care system. It's not a case of children being removed to supply an adoption need. Targets are for finding forever families for children who need them, not the other way around. In fact, it's a relatively tiny percentage of all looked-after children (around 5%) who are adopted each year.

A 2007 study carried out for the British Association for Adoption and Fostering (BAAF) found that 41% of people believed that mothers put up their children for adoption at birth. Only 29% of those who answered knew that most children in need of new homes had suffered from neglect or abuse.

Neglect and abuse

A large number of the children awaiting adoption in the UK have suffered some form of neglect or abuse within their birth family set-up.

This abuse may have been emotional, physical or sexual and because this tends to happen behind locked doors, children are usually over the age of one by the time they are approved for adoption.

Sometimes, when a birth family has had their older children removed and freed for adoption, their younger babies will enter the care system a lot quicker as there will be pre-existing concerns over the birth parents' abilities to keep their children safe and well.

Children who have experienced abuse and neglect deal with it in a huge range of ways; there are themes and common experiences but each child is different. As much as you can try to prepare yourself mentally, coping with the weight of your adoptive child's history can be incredibly tough and it's essential that you seek as much help and support as possible.

This is where other adopters can be a lifeline!

'As much as you can try to prepare yourself mentally, coping with the weight of your adoptive child's history can be incredibly tough and it's essential that you seek as much help and support as possible.'

Differences between fostering and adoption

In a nutshell, adoption is for life, whereas fostering provides a temporary placement for a child. Children may need fostering for short periods due to their main carers being ill, in prison or hospital for example (there is more about fostering in chapter 2).

Adoption is forever and children will only be made available for adoption when there is no chance of them returning safely to their birth families.

Adoption and Children Act 2002

In 2002, the most radical shake-up of UK adoption laws for 26 years was finally fully implemented. The new act, subtitled 'Every Child Matters', replaced the outdated Adoption Act 1976 and finally modernised adoption from home and abroad.

It also brought in a new term you may have heard: special guardianship. Special guardianship is a form of legal permanence for children not suitable for adoption.

Special guardianship gives the guardian parental responsibility, while the child's biological parents also keep parental responsibility – although their ability to use this is very limited.

Why would special guardianship be awarded?

There are a number of reasons, but it could be because a child is older and has said they do not wish to be officially adopted.

It could be because the child is in long-term foster care or is being cared for on a permanent basis by other members of the birth family. In some cases, the child or their carer may have religious or cultural issues with adoption.

FAQs

How long does the adoption process take?

Frustrating as it is to hear – how long is a piece of string? It really does depend on your circumstances, whether the local or voluntary agency is short of social work staff, whether it is an adoption from within your family and whether the birth parents of the child you are matched with are trying to block the adoption going ahead. That said, a rough guide is around two years in total.

It is likely to take no less than eight months from your first call to the adoption agency to the approval panel. But as many adopters and prospective adopters will tell you, it can be a lot longer. Once you've been approved, being matched to a child can take anything from a few weeks to several years.

I have birth children already, will this matter?

Having birth children will not disqualify, nor automatically qualify, you for adoption. There will be considerations though, such as appropriate age gaps. Some social workers will not want to place adoptive children who are older than existing birth children.

Do I need to be British?

You don't have to have been born in the UK to adopt here. You can apply to adopt if your permanent home is in the UK or you have been a resident here for over a year – and you have solid proof of this.

Will the child take my surname?

Once the adoption is finalised, your adopted child is legally a part of your family, and normally this includes taking the family surname. Sometimes, particularly in older children, the birth surname can be incorporated as a middle name.

Can I adopt a baby?

There are some babies in need of adoptive families, but the average age of children at adoption is four years and one month. There are more older children than babies who need new parents.

As stated in *Adopting a Child – A Guide for People Interested in Adoption* by Jennifer Lord, between March 2004 and March 2005, only 210 babies under one were adopted in England, of the 3,800 total looked-after-children who were adopted.

Can I adopt from abroad?

It is possible to adopt children from abroad; however you do still need to follow certain procedures. You will find more information on this in chapter 3.

How much will adoption cost?

Adopting a child from within the UK shouldn't cost very much. You may need to pay for references, medicals and certificates, but we're not talking hundreds and hundreds of pounds.

If you are on a very low income or benefits, you may be able to ask for fees to be waived or reduced. It's best to have a chat with your social worker about this.

Adoption from abroad can cost several thousand pounds, depending on where you are searching for your child. At the very least, you will normally need to pay the agency who handles your home study – BAAF suggests this will be around £4,000. Local Authorities (LAs) must prioritise the placement of children from within the UK and will charge to reflect this.

Can I adopt more than one child at a time?

You can adopt a sibling group rather than just one child, in fact more adopters are needed who are willing to adopt groups of sisters and brothers and many agencies will be very keen to hear from you.

Adopting more than one child means having to provide the space, attention and specialised care that each child needs. There is a lot to think about practically as well, such as a big enough car, enough bedrooms and the finances!

Sibling groups truly benefit from staying together and sharing comfort and support. Over half the children waiting to be adopted are in sibling groups and the majority need to stay together.

Sadly some groups of siblings (especially four or more) will be separated and adopted separately if no suitable adopters are found for the whole group. In this instance, ongoing contact between the siblings will be considered by the agency that places them with forever families.

'Over half the children waiting to be adopted are in sibling groups and the majority need to stay together.'

Summing Up

Your head is probably spinning with all the factors you'll need to consider! Don't worry, this is perfectly normal and every prospective adopter will have felt overwhelmed and daunted at times during their journey from thinking about adoption to welcoming their new child into their lives.

The adoption process is far fairer now than ever before, and while it can feel like the wheels are turning incredibly slowly, this does give you plenty of time to think, plan, discuss and come to terms with all the changes that are around the corner.

Chapter Two

Fostering

Fostering in the UK

If you don't currently have anything to do with the world of fostering and adoption, you may not be aware of the full scale of the care system in the UK.

According to the British Association for Adoption and Fostering (BAAF), some 60,000 children were in the care of Local Authorities (LAs) (looked after children) on 31 March 2007 and 71% of them were living within foster placements.

According to BAAF, as at 31 March 2007, the ages of children in care could be broken down like this:

- 5% (3,000) of children were under one.

- 15% (8,800) were aged between one and four-years-old.

- 18% (10,900) were aged between five and nine-years-old.

- 42% (25,500) were aged between 10 and 15-years-old.

- 20% (11,800) were aged 16 and over.

A large proportion of these children – over 10,000 – are from Muslim, Asian, Black and Ethnic communities. Foster carers from these communities are in short supply.

Who manages foster care?

Local Authorities (LAs) all have fostering teams who manage the foster care scenario in the local area. There are also independent fostering agencies, which work alongside LAs.

Your first point of call should always be your local agency. You should be able to find details of your LA in the phone book. Alternatively, the Adoption UK website (www.adoptionuk.org) has a 'Find an Agency' section.

Who can foster?

The criteria for foster carers is a little broader than for adopters, although rules are still strict.

- Foster carers must be 18 or over.

- There is no upper age limit, although most carers are under 60 when they start fostering.

- People of all sexualities, races and religions can apply.

- Single people, married couples, civil partners, co-habiting couples, separated and divorced people can all apply to be foster carers.

- People with birth children can apply.

- Your existing job or any other factors such as disabilities will be looked at on a case-by-case basis.

- Any criminal records must be declared, but may not automatically disqualify you for consideration.

- You must be able to demonstrate that you can communicate well with children and are responsible, caring and energetic enough to cope with the demands of a young child or several children.

Why do children need fostering?

Children need foster care because their birth parents can't look after them at that time. This can be for all sorts of reasons and can affect children from varied backgrounds.

A fostering placement tends to fall into one of these categories:

- Emergency care – when children need a safe home for a couple of nights.

- Short-term care – this tends to cover a few weeks to a few months and can happen in the run-up to a longer placement within the care system or a return to the birth family.

- Short breaks – respite breaks for disabled, special needs or challenging children, to give some space and time for their parents or carers. This tends to be arranged in advance and can be a regular occurrence.

- Kinship care – looking after children from within your family (or looking after friends' children).

- Long-term foster care – this can be very similar to adoption and is often used for older children who continue to see birth relatives regularly.

- Remand fostering – this occurs when the court remands young people into the care of a foster carer who has been specially trained to handle this type of placement. This only applies to England and Wales; Scotland does not use the same system.

- Private fostering – this is a private arrangement between those with parental responsibility and a private foster carer who is not a close relative nor has parental responsibilities for the child. The stay is a private arrangement that lasts over 27 days and the LA will need to be informed so they can visit to check on the child's welfare.

Sometimes, birth parents need a bit of space and time to sort out their own problems or to put some space between them and a child whose behaviour is extremely challenging. So long as the child is considered to be safe, they can return to their birth home after living with the foster carer.

How long would I foster each child for?

Each fostering placement is unique and any foster carer will tell you that a few weeks can become a fair bit longer. The type of placement, for example emergency, should give you an indication of how long the child will live within your home.

Are foster carers paid?

Foster carers are entitled to allowances to cover the costs of caring for children in their home. There are also additional allowances given for special occasions like birthdays. There are minimum allowances, but no upper cap. The amounts paid depend on the age of the child and the area where you live.

The Fostering Network, a charity devoted to everyone involved in foster care, has been calling for fairer allowances for years. They claim that in many cases the money paid just doesn't cover everything a foster family needs day-to-day.

The DCSF (formerly DfES) National Minimum Fostering Allowances per week for England in 2007–08 were:

Region	Babies	Pre-primary school	Primary school age	Secondary school age (11–15)	Secondary school age (16–17)
Base (£)	100	102	113	129	151
South East (£)	111	114	127	144	169
London (£)	116	119	132	150	176

Registered, experienced foster carers can work for independent fostering agencies with more challenging placements, which generally pay more.

Scotland

There are national standards laid down for the provision of pay to be awarded to foster carers in Scotland. The standards say: 'you can be confident that you receive payments to cover the cost of caring for any children or young people placed with you. Payments are based on their needs and in line with the cost of caring for them.' These are covered in Standard 9 of the National Care Standards for Foster Care and Family Placement Services (which can be found on the website, www.scotland.gov.uk) and Regulation 9 of the Fostering of Children (Scotland) Regulations 1996 (see www.legislation.hmso.gov.uk).

Wales

The Welsh Assembly government is currently working on a set of national minimum fostering allowances but, at the time of going to press, the requirements for foster carer payments in Wales are covered in Standard 30 of the National Minimum Standards for Fostering Services. More can be found out at www.wales.gov.uk.

Northern Ireland

The trusts in Northern Ireland pay standard allowances according to a Model Scheme, which was drawn up along with the four Health and Social Services Boards.

For the full list, see www.dhsspsni.gov.uk/hss/fostering and click on 'allowances'

Tax relief

In 2003, tax relief was introduced for foster carers in the UK. This means carers do not pay tax on income from fostering up to a maximum of £10,000 a year plus allowances.

National insurance contributions

Also in 2003, foster carers became entitled to Home Responsibility Protection, which means that carers will not miss out on the basic retirement pension because of staying at home caring for children, rather than working in traditional forms of employment outside of the home.

How do I apply to become a foster carer?

Firstly, you need to speak to your LA. Give them a call and ask to speak to their fostering team. You could also apply to a neighbouring LA, but agencies do prefer to place children for fostering as close to their home area as possible.

Initially, you need to have a chat about fostering in the area and how to apply to become a carer. You will then be invited to a group session in your area where you can meet other prospective foster carers and learn more about the children in care and the challenges you will face.

You will need to be police-checked and probably have a medical examination to ensure you're fit and healthy enough to cope with looking after children. The fostering agency will also complete a formal report, which will be presented to the agency's fostering panel.

Who is on the fostering panel?

Like an adoption approval panel, the fostering panel will consist of up to 10 people. The panellists will include social workers, independent people and at least one foster carer. You can choose to attend the panel, which can be particularly helpful to the panellists who may want to ask you questions.

Approval

The panel will make a recommendation on whether you should be allowed to become a foster carer. This recommendation is then passed to the senior manager of the fostering agency who will make the ultimate decision. The whole application process will take around six months in England, Wales and Scotland.

What happens next?

Once you are approved as a foster carer, the fostering agency will make a foster care agreement with you. This agreement covers what is expected of you, as a carer, and of the agency. It will also include the legal requirement that foster carers are never allowed to smack the children in their care.

Foster carers need to be able to work alongside social workers, birth parents or their families, schools and other professionals. When a child is first placed with you, it will be really beneficial to keep as much of their familiar routine as possible. Birth relatives' knowledge is a real boon here – from learning about food tastes, favourite toys, hobbies and fears, through to health concerns and development issues. The more you can find out, the more consistent the care you can provide – and the less jolts the child will feel.

Of course, sadly, some children will be coming from a situation where they were in danger or receiving inconsistent or unsafe care, and it will not always be possible – or appropriate – to recreate much of their home-life.

There is paperwork!

The fostering agency will need to keep track of which child is placed with which carer. There will be a placement agreement between you and the agency for each child placed. This will cover the basics like the date of the placement through to the child's medical needs, contact with birth relatives and any financial support to be provided.

You will be visited regularly by the child's social workers, but also from social workers within your fostering agency. Your supervising social worker is there to support and help you.

As for training, you can keep on learning for as long as you're a foster carer!

A programme of regular training should be offered by your agency and some will offer social events for foster families in the area.

Placement reviews

The child placed in your care will have regular reviews from social workers to find out how they are doing. These happen a month after placement, then a further three months on and every three months after that.

Ongoing approval

Even though you will have been approved to foster, this will need to be reviewed every year. This may sound scary, but it's a real opportunity to bring up support you felt was needed and any concerns that you have.

'Foster carers need to be able to work alongside social workers, birth parents or their families, schools and other professionals.'

Summing Up

- Any adult from any background (except those with certain criminal records) can apply to be a foster carer.

- Fostering provides a safe home for children who, for all sorts of reasons, cannot live with their birth families.

- The placements can last from a couple of days to long-term, over several years.

- You will need to be approved by your fostering agency and agree to certain conditions and ongoing assessments.

- You may have direct or indirect contact with the child's birth family and, if the child goes on to be adopted by another family, you may have a chance to speak with the adopter or adopters about the child and their lifestyle.

- You and your placements will be routinely reviewed but this should be an opportunity to ask for more support if you need it.

Chapter Three

Why Consider Adoption?

Reasons to adopt

Infertility

According to the Human Fertility and Embryology Authority, in 2005, 32,626 people in the UK were receiving infertility treatment, with 11,262 babies being born as a result.

Around 3.5 million people – one in seven UK couples – is thought to experience fertility problems. In fact, infertility is the commonest reason for women aged 20-45 to see their GP, after pregnancy itself.

IVF success rates decrease the higher the woman's age and sadly not all treatments are successful. And, of course, many couples who experience fertility issues do not opt to go down the IVF route and may look into the possibilities of adoption.

Your adoption agency will need to be sure that you have properly grieved for any unsuccessful IVF attempts and any lost pregnancies. Some agencies will also have a set period of time that they will want to have elapsed (normally six months to a year) between your last IVF treatment and an application to adopt.

'Around 3.5 million people – one in seven UK couples – is thought to experience fertility problems. In fact, infertility is the commonest reason for women aged 20-45 to see their GP, after pregnancy itself.'

Altruism

Some people are keen to adopt rather than conceive birth children because they wish to give an existing child a loving home. Social workers will want to explore your reasons for adopting and ensure that you have a realistic idea of the rigours of accepting a new child into your home.

The reality is, it's not just about giving a child in need a lot of love. In many cases, love and affection are secondary to routine, safety and structure. However, it's not hard to see why people want to adopt, regardless of being able to have birth children.

There are around 60,000 children in the UK care system at any time and many of these children will experience multiple homes in their young and fragmented lives. In 2005, it was reported in *The Times* newspaper that some children in care are moved as many as 20 times because a permanent family cannot be found.

'Many mums and dads with existing birth children and step-families consider adoption as a way to grow their family.'

Multiple moves break up brothers and sisters, disrupt education and can be incredibly damaging to children's ability to form secure attachments throughout life. Department of Health figures suggest that over 600 babies experience three or more placements every single year.

Adoption creates and grows families, but it is not simple and it is not just about love or patience. This will need to be explored as part of your home study.

Growing your existing family

Many mums and dads with existing birth children and step-families consider adoption as a way to grow their family. Sometimes this can also be due to infertility, altruism or sometimes a combination.

Social workers will need to know the full history of your existing children – and will want to talk to any ex-partners with whom you have had children – and you'll need to show you have considered existing children's needs and the needs of any potential children.

Many agencies will want you to think carefully about age gaps – a lot of them will not be comfortable placing a child who is older than your birth children as this can be even more disruptive for all the children.

Depending on the age of your children, they may be interviewed by the social worker who is conducting your home study – a good social worker will be gentle and caring in the way they approach this and you will have a chance to talk to them about any concerns beforehand.

Who can adopt?

Am I too old?

Adopters in England and Wales need to be over 21 to apply, but there is no upper age limit. The most important thing is that you are healthy and energetic enough to cope with the demands of a child.

Some agencies have a cap on the age gap between adopters and children (often 40 to 45 years) but this is not a blanket rule.

Do I need to be married?

No. Following the Adoption and Children Act 2002, unmarried couples and those in a same sex relationship are allowed to adopt alongside single people and married couples.

Can I still work?

In theory, yes, you can keep working but ideally one parent will give up work, at least temporarily. Where there are two parents, finding a way for both of you to spend as much time at home as possible is recommended. Perhaps one of you could work condensed hours, for example? Or work one day a week from home?

Children who are adopted have all experienced loss of some kind, even those who have had a relatively smooth early life and consistent foster care. In the early days as a new family, they – and you – will be experiencing such a rollercoaster of change that as much continuity as possible will pay dividends. As with any new parent, taking as much time to bond with your new child will pay dividends for you and for them.

If your adoptive child is of school age and you find you have enough time during these hours, part-time work could be a very sensible option but this really does depend on the child's needs.

It's often hard to gauge the true extent that you will be needed at home until your new family is living day-to-day under the same roof. Of course this is easier said than done; bills need to be paid and there is absolutely no shame in wanting some adult company and a sense of career fulfilment, but, if possible, try to reach a balance that suits the whole family.

Flexible-working

As an employee who has worked over 26 weeks for your employers, you have a right to request flexible work arrangements and your employer must consider these fairly.

You can make this request once you are responsible for a child under six or a disabled child under 18. Your employer is legally obliged to seriously consider your application, although they can turn it down if there is a good business reason.

Do I need to own my own home?

You don't need to be a homeowner to be considered for adoption, but you will need to show that you have enough space in your home to accommodate a child – and all the clothes, toys and bits and bobs that a child needs!

Agencies do like you to have a spare bedroom available, however it could be acceptable for an adopted child to share with an existing child within your family. If this is an idea you're considering, your existing child must be happy with this and you may need to show that you have a back-up plan if this doesn't remain a harmonious situation!

Do you need to be rich?

Being rich is certainly not essential. Adoption agencies will need to see that you can support yourself and your family, but you do not need to live in a palace! You can be a homeowner, council tenant or private tenant – it's all acceptable.

If money is tight, you may receive some financial help to pay for your growing family's costs.

Religion and culture

As you can probably imagine, this is a thorny issue with a chequered history!

Children of all cultural and religious backgrounds are awaiting forever families, while adopters of all strands of culture and religion are hopeful for adoptive children. Sadly, as neat as it would be, the numbers and circumstances don't always mirror each other and there is a disproportionate number of non-white children waiting for new parents.

Agencies are keen to find parents whose own ethnic make-up complements the child and where culture and religion can be acknowledged, explored and celebrated within the home.

The Adoption and Children Act 2002 said that a placing agency 'must give due consideration to the child's religious persuasion, racial origin and cultural and linguistic background.' This does not mean that parents with different backgrounds to children will not be considered, but careful consideration will need to be shown for how cultural heritage can be positively promoted within the family.

If you're looking to adopt a child from a different ethnic background to yourself, it can really help to have some connections to that community through friends, relatives or the area you live in.

Will a criminal record prevent me from adopting?

If you or your partner or spouse has a criminal record, you must tell the adoption agency or LA when applying. A criminal record does not automatically disqualify you, but if you, your partner or a member of your household has been convicted or cautioned for an offence against a child, then the law will not permit you to adopt or foster children.

I'm a smoker, will this affect my application?

Under the new Adoption and Children Act 2002, agencies can't have blanket bans on any one group of people – this includes smokers. However, your health and lifestyle will be taken into account, as will the risks of passive smoking.

It is very wise to give up smoking – which is an impressive act in itself and shows a commitment to your plans for a family – or at the very least ban all smoking in the home.

Do I need experience with kids?

You may be asked to demonstrate your experience of spending time with children, especially children within the age range you'd like to adopt.

Think about time spent with young relatives but also consider getting hands-on experience with a local playgroup, school or youth group. Many are crying out for help but you will need to be CRB (Criminal Records Bureau) approved. You can arrange this yourself proactively – for more information go to www.crb.gov. uk.

The website www.do-it.org.uk has listings of available volunteering posts. Or you can speak to the organisation you'd like to volunteer with and they should be able to help you.

Tick list

- Sexuality, marital status, homeowner status and religion are not barriers to applying to adopt.

- Anyone over the age of 21 can apply to adopt.

- You need to have the means to take care of yourself and your growing family, but you do not need to be rich.

- You or your partner must declare a criminal record.

- Your social worker will want to explore how you intend to manage work and you may need to make provisions for reducing hours or taking extended time off.

- You may need to demonstrate experience with children – but there are plenty of volunteering roles where you can spend valuable time with youngsters.

International adoption

Around 300 children every year are brought to the UK from overseas and adopted to live here. Adopting a family from overseas is a huge topic with its own challenges, complicated legislation and special considerations, so please take this section as an introduction only!

First steps

The first step is to contact your LA or a voluntary adoption agency just as you would for a domestic adoption. You still need to go through these channels and be fully approved before you can adopt from abroad. Your agency's social worker will be able to talk you through the process fully.

You will need to be approved for suitability to adopt by the agency's adoption panel and the final approval decision falls to a senior manager in the agency – the 'agency decision maker'. Once you've been approved to adopt a child from another country, your application will be sent to the Department for Children, Schools and Families (DCSF).

The government agency, DCSF, is responsible for processing all intercountry adoption applications from UK residents. They'll check that your application meets all the relevant UK laws but also the laws and specific requirements of the country you'd like to adopt from. While your application is being processed, the DCSF should keep you informed of your case's progress in writing.

'Adoption is not a straightforward process – and there are many different forms!'

The DCSF process

The DCSF process is outlined in the following seven steps:

1. The DCSF will receive the case from the adoption agency. They will then let adopters know they have received this.

2. A DCSF caseworker will look through the paperwork and check that everything is there. If any information is missing or out of date they will let the agency know so it can be amended or replaced.

3. When the DCSF is happy with the paperwork and is satisfied that the prospective adopters have been properly assessed and approved to UK standards and to meet the other country's regulations, they will issue a Certificate of Eligibility and Suitability to Adopt and let the adopters know this has happened.

4. A DCSF caseworker will send the paperwork to a Notary Public (chosen by the prospective adopters). Not all countries will need the papers to be notarised though.

5. The Notary Public will normally send the papers back to the DCSF casework team. The papers will then be legalised at the Foreign and Commonwealth Office if the other country requires this.

6. The Foreign and Commonwealth Office will send the papers back to the DCSF casework team. They will then be sent on to the other country's Embassy in London for the final stage of legalisation.

7. The Embassy will return the papers to the DCSF and the application will then be sent to the relevant agency or contact in the other country.

Please visit www.dcsf.gov.uk for further information.

Things to consider

- Intercountry adoption is a long and protracted process, mainly because you're dealing with two countries' laws, working practices and – in some cases – languages. It's not a quick route!
- You will need to have thought about which country you'd like to adopt from and why.

- It's important to consider how you will keep your adopted child aware of their 'roots' and birth culture.

- Will you learn to speak the native tongue of your child's birth country?

Kinship adoption

Historically, older relatives within some households would adopt the offspring of young, unmarried relatives and raise children as their own.

In some cases, big sisters turned out to be birth mothers and mothers turned out to be grandmothers. This is now very rare, especially as adoption becomes more open and unmarried and very young mothers are no longer stigmatised – at least to such a degree.

A small percentage of adoptions each year do happen within the birth family, however. When children can no longer be safely raised by their birth parents, LAs will look to the wider birth family to see if a placement can be made. By placing a child within their wider kinship network, more about their young lives can be kept consistent. In many cultures kinship adoption is very common, for example in Japan where adoption of non-relatives is rare.

Of course, kinship adoption is not a golden ticket to a painless experience – in many ways there are more considerations and loose ends.

'By placing a child within their wider kinship network, more about their young lives can be kept consistent.'

Summing Up

- Adoption is not a straightforward process – and there are many different forms!

- Whether you're planning to adopt from the UK, from overseas or from within your own extended family, the first point of call is always your LA or voluntary adoption agency.

- There will be a head-spinning amount of things to think about – considerations you'd probably never realised existed! It's fine to be overwhelmed and it's fine to take the time to really digest everything you have learned and everything you may need to make a decision about.

Chapter Four

Early Enquiries and the Application Process

Local or voluntary agency

Adoptions in the UK are conducted through LAs or voluntary agencies. Unlike in the US, popularised by shows like *Friends*, private adoption is not the norm.

Your first steps into adoption should be a call to your LA's adoption team. You can ask about the ages of children in the area, the process and give the team some details about you and your current situation. From there, they will be able to tell you how to continue to apply and what the local process (and possible timescale) is.

You are not duty bound to adopt through your LA though.

Voluntary adoption agencies

Voluntary Agencies (or VAs as they're sometimes known) tend to specialise in adoption and fostering. Generally, they are smaller than LA teams but often cover a wider area, unrestricted by wards and council areas.

The majority of VAs have charitable status. According to the Consortium of Voluntary Adoption Agencies, one in five of all looked after adopted children join families recruited by VAs.

Many VAs originated from church-run organisations or children's charities. Barnado's, for example, was started by Thomas Barnado in 1867 after he witnessed the terrible numbers of destitute children living on the streets in Victorian London.

The charity set up children's homes and schemes for helping unmarried mothers. Over the years, this has evolved away from institutions and into the arena of adoption. Now Barnado's runs a voluntary fostering and adoption agency.

Why consider a voluntary agency?

Some prospective adopters believe the service will be better and more personal – but every agency is different and it's good to get first hand opinions on the options near to you.

VAs often specialise in placing children that are considered likely to need ongoing support.

Concurrent planning

Concurrent planning has gained in popularity in recent years, though it is still fairly controversial and certainly not for everyone.

Concurrent planning sees a baby removed from their birth parents and placed with prospective adopters. Meanwhile, the baby's birth parents are encouraged and supported to overcome challenges that affect their ability to provide their child with a safe home.

Good enough?

The key phrase is 'good enough parenting' – the birth parents do not need to prove they are impeccable, amazing parents, but that they can provide a safe, 'good enough' home. This can be very hard to swallow for potential adopters who feel they can provide far better than simply good enough.

'The majority of VAs have charitable status. According to the Consortium of Voluntary Adoption Agencies, one in five of all looked after adopted children join families recruited by VAs.'

Infants who are living in a concurrent planning situation are not just placed with any prospective adopters. Special training and careful consideration is given to the adopters and the set-up is more akin to fostering, where the placement is intended to last around six to nine months.

During this time, the birth family are given intensive support but if it is not possible to return the child to the birth home, full adoption will go ahead. The vast majority of concurrency planning cases do result in adoption, but it is certainly not a 'done deal' and this must be considered.

The concept of concurrent planning started in the US and filtered over to the UK in the 1990s, headed up by the work of the Coram Family charity (www. coram.org.uk).

Things to think about

You will be asked to make some tough decisions about the child you could see yourself parenting.

You will need to consider which age range you would hope for, ethnicity, gender, physical or mental disabilities and if you feel you could cope with parenting a child with a history of abuse. You will also be asked to consider the number of children you would like to adopt.

You may change your mind completely from your initial feelings and find yourself wanting to welcome an older child, having always imagined a baby joining your family. You may consider a sibling group or a single child and you may decide you can provide the support and parenting that a disabled child may need.

Initial application

If you decide you wish to formerly apply to adopt, you will probably be invited to attend a local information meeting held by your chosen agency. Here you will have the chance to learn more about the process, meet with agency staff and other prospective adopters.

'You will be asked to make some tough decisions about the child you could see yourself parenting.'

Often you will also get the chance to pick the brains of foster carers and adoptive parents – make the most of it! These are the people who live adoption and fostering 24/7 and can give you the most accurate, honest idea of what awaits.

Preparation groups

Once you have formally applied, you will be invited to between six and eight preparation groups held by your agency.

The sessions will cover:

- Reasons children enter the care system.
- Legal adoption processes.
- Behaviours caused by neglect or abuse.
- Child development – mental, emotional and physical.
- Attachment issues.
- Meeting and understanding children's needs.
- Understanding the experiences (separation, loss and trauma) which affect adopted children.
- Issues surrounding identity.
- Settling children into a new home.
- Contact and its forms (direct, indirect) with birth families and foster carers.
- Post-adoption support.

Mixing with a group of strangers isn't everyone's cup of tea, but the local preparation groups are incredibly important and can provide you with new friends who know exactly what you are going through while you follow your adoption journey. You may get the chance to speak with adopters, adopted adults and sometimes even a birth parent.

Go without prejudice; you may meet friends for life and you may come out with a new way of thinking and tips for surviving the sometimes lengthy and gruelling journey.

'Mixing with a group of strangers isn't everyone's cup of tea, but the local preparation groups are incredibly important and can provide you with new friends who know exactly what you are going through while you follow your adoption journey.'

Assessment

A social worker from the agency you're applying through will be assigned to come to your home several times and get to know you better – this will happen over several months in small doses.

They will ask very searching questions and you may feel uncomfortable at first. However, it is an invaluable process for getting any issues out in the open, for discussing you and your partner's feelings and for letting your social worker get to know you, your relationships, your home, and to be able to represent all of this to the panel who ultimately decide if you will be allowed to adopt.

You'll be asked about your own family background and your childhood. This can be a very emotional journey, whether you considered yours a happy childhood or not, and this is fine.

Frank discussions and tough questions

You will need to be frank about your current circumstances: have you tried other avenues to have a family? Have you fully grieved for any lost children or unsuccessful IVF attempts? Are you still hoping to have a birth child at some stage?

Every member of your household will be talked to, although children and elderly members of the household will be handled gently and appropriately.

References

As part of the homestudy, two references of your choice will be interviewed. They will be asked about your relationship if you have a partner and your ability to resolve conflict and deal with stress.

They will be asked questions they may find uncomfortable, such as if they feel a child could be in danger in your home or if you have ever presented yourself as violent or aggressive. This is only ever for the best interests of the child you may adopt, it is not intended as a judgement or an accusation.

Children and ex-partners

If you have birth children with a previous partner, they will be asked similar questions. This is a relatively new requirement and can cause discomfort. However, if an ex-partner had ever experienced violence or abuse, for example, it is vital that social workers are aware of this. As hard and humiliating as some prospective adopters find it, it is for valid reasons.

Medicals

You will need a full medical examination from your own GP and he or she will then give a report to your agency's medical advisor. The report will cover both your own and your family's medical history.

The agency's advisor will then assess the health implications of adoption – will your health be up to the challenge of a young child? Are there any known conditions which will considerably shorten your life expectancy?

Written report – the Form F

Everything that the social worker asks from you will help him or her to create the official form – Form F. This is the official form which is completed for every adopter and it contains two parts.

The first part of the Form F covers the more basic factual information, including the sort of child you would consider adopting (hence the importance of considering this properly, as already mentioned).

The second part of the form is the assessment part and contains the social worker's observations about you and your family, your home and profile.

It can feel very odd to read about yourself and someone's filtered version of your life! Sometimes it can be a very enlightening experience, but sometimes you may not entirely agree with the way you've been presented. It's important you discuss this with your social worker and request any changes.

The final version of the Form F will be presented to the adoption panel (more on this later) so it is important you have a chance to iron out any creases.

Summing Up

The application process is long, emotionally tiring and intrusive. This probably sounds like Hell!

However, there are very good reasons for the intrusion and it is just as essential for you that everyone working to match you with a child has the best possible idea of who you are and the life you lead.

You will need to provide references – including ex-partners with whom you have birth children – and they may be surprised by some of the searching questions that will be put to them.

A social worker from your adoption agency will visit your home and talk to you individually and if you are in a relationship, as a couple.

The social worker's findings and opinions, plus your background information and the type of child you would like to parent, will be written up into a standard form called the Form F. This will be presented to an adoption panel for approval and will be used by social workers when matching you with a specific child.

An overview of the application process

- Make initial contact with an agency.
- Attend an information meeting held by the agency.
- Visits from agency social worker in your home.
- Formal application.
- Police and medical checks.
- Preparation and training.
- Home study.
- Adoption panel.
- Official agency approval.
- Begin to search for a child.

'The application process is long, emotionally tiring and intrusive. This probably sounds like Hell!'

Chapter Five

Managing Expectations

Length of process

Annoying as it is to hear, the old adage 'how long is a piece of string?' really comes into play here.

The time it can take to assess you varies from area to area, agency to agency and even social worker to social worker. The old chestnuts of staff shortages and waiting lists rear their ugly heads and it can be wise to 'shop around' before settling on the agency you wish to apply through.

The recommended maximum time from formal application is eight months (seven months in Scotland), but this is just a guide. Once you have been approved it can then be weeks, months or even years before a suitable match with a child comes up.

Often, it's not your own expectations about timescale that causes feelings of frustration – after all, you will hopefully have heard the low-down on this at your preparation groups. No, it's often your over-zealous friends and family who know what a great parent you'll be and wonder why it's taking everyone else so long to realise it!

Try and gently explain to them that there is a set process and it does take time, partly because fast-tracking it would rush you when it's actually very important that you get to digest everything you're learning and feeling.

You will have the rest of your lives with the child you adopt and it's essential that you go into the process as prepared as possible, even if it can seem like everyone is dragging their heels!

'Once you have been approved it can then be weeks, months or even years before a suitable match with a child comes up.'

Children's histories

Similar to your Form F, each child being released for adoption will have a Child Permanence Report (CPR, formerly known as a Form E). The report contains information about the child, a profile of their medical and emotional needs, their birth family background and their present situation.

Thanks to the Adoption and Children Act 2002, prospective adopters now have the right to see detailed information in the CPR. This is to help you get the best possible picture of the child you are being matched with, and should make it easier for you to decide if you would like to proceed or find out more.

It's never an easy decision to say no, especially when you've waited so long, but it is far, far better to say no to a potential match at this stage, than further down the line.

'The average age of children freed for adoption is actually just over four-years-old. The wait for younger babies is longer than for toddlers and upwards.'

Average ages of children available for adoption

Although soap story lines tend to feature babies given up for adoption, this is incredibly rare. The average age of children freed for adoption is actually just over four-years-old. The wait for younger babies is longer than for toddlers and upwards.

Medical challenges

All children released for adoption will have had a thorough medical and development assessment. This will have been done by a paediatrician and will also look at the health of the birth mother during pregnancy (including whether drug or alcohol use occurred), any known medical history of the birth family (including genetic disorders and inherited conditions) and the details of the birth father's medical and family history – if known.

It's not always possible to detect future medical problems and there are no guarantees. But then, there is no guarantee with any child.

Emotional challenges

Emotional challenges – both current and future – are far harder to detect than physical challenges.

For a start, children can present one way when they're in the foster carer's home and quite another when they are living in a new home that has been introduced to them as their forever family.

It's important to have an open mind and soak up as much 'real life' experience as you can lay your hands on! Speaking to existing adopters is really the best way to get the real inside scoop on the likely emotional challenges – so grab any opportunities, such as training courses or preparation groups, where you can meet adopters with both hands!

Arranging and preparing for long-term support

More on this later, because it's very important!

None of us know what the future holds, but the more open, honest and comprehensive the information you're given during matching, the more likely you are to ask for the support you will need.

We'll talk more about post-adoption support from your agency in chapter 14, but don't forget that support comes in many forms.

The support of your friends, family and colleagues will help see you through the challenges and emotional ups and downs of the adoption process and your life as an adoptive family.

Even the most straightforward adoption is a huge life shift for you; no matter how thrilled you are and how ready you have felt, no-one is immune to shock and panic! Having friends to call on to keep you grounded and supported can not be underestimated.

The friends that you meet at your preparation groups can be great, as they are in a similar boat, but sometimes it's your oldest friends that you need to chat with, reminding yourself that adoption and the adoptive process is not the only thing that defines you, that you are still you. Laughing is exceptionally important!

'Emotional challenges – both current and future – are far harder to detect than physical challenges.'

Summing Up

Managing your and your family's expectations about adoption and the child available for adoption is very important. There are many shades of grey – children's ages may not match with your imagined family (babies are very rarely available for adoption) and sibling groups are in much need of a forever family. You may not have considered disabled children or those with special needs.

Your social worker will talk to you about all these considerations and more, but it's easy to feel bewildered and overwhelmed. This is normal – some of the reasons children end up in need of adoption are bewildering and overwhelming; abuse, neglect and disability are not easy topics.

It's very important that you take the time to think about all these considerations, but that you also take time to look after yourself, to consider what you could really manage day-to-day, month-by-month, year-by-year.

Your support network – both formal (via your agency, the law) and informal (friends, family, colleagues, membership charities like Adoption UK) – can give you the space to relax, take advice, take stock and sometimes have a little scream!

'Your support network – both formal and informal – can give you the space to relax, take advice, take stock and sometimes have a little scream!'

Chapter Six

Approval

The approval panel

Who is on the approval panel?

Your agency's adoption panel will be made up of around 10 people, all of whom are there to consider and advise on the following:

- Whether a looked-after child should be released for adoption.

- Whether you, as a prospective adopter, should be approved to adopt.

- Whether you, as approved adopters who have been matched with a child, are suitable to adopt that child (more on this later).

The panellists will be a mixture of social workers, agency managers and a medical expert, as well as a possible combination of foster carers, adoptive parents, adult adoptees and other professionals such as teachers.

What happens at the panel?

Your home study assessment report – which you will have had a chance to see and comment on – will have been sent to all the panel members before the panel meeting. Usually they'll have had at least a couple of weeks to look over the information and get a thorough idea of the details of your application.

It's very likely that many of the panel members will have questions about some of the report – perhaps they may want to know a little more about your choices, your plans or your background. Don't worry if you don't feel comfortable answering these questions; they are usually put to your social worker who put together the report.

They may wish to ask you questions directly, but don't worry, they're experienced people who know how nervous you are!

When the panel have finished asking questions, they will discuss the application in private and reach a decision. This does not mean you have been approved or declined; it is a recommendation that the agency's senior decision maker will base their decision on – but it's a pretty good indicator!

What happens if I am approved?

If the panel feels you would be a suitable adoptive parent, or parents, they will say so. They will also approve the age range and type of child they would be happy to see you adopt.

The agency's decision maker – normally a senior manager – will then make the final decision based, in part, on the panel's recommendation. You will then shortly receive a letter notifying you of your formal approval.

This is the first of several milestones when you can crack out the Champagne and treat yourself to a night off from worrying and waiting for the next hurdle!

And now the waiting game starts…

After the excitement of approval, the period that follows can seem a real anti-climax. This is a very good time to try and book a holiday or at least a couple of days of relaxation and fun somewhere.

It may seem like nothing is happening, but behind the scenes your social worker will be looking at a possible child to match you with. More on this in the next chapter.

'After the excitement of approval, the period that follows can seem a real anti-climax. This is a very good time to try and book a holiday or at least a couple of days of relaxation and fun somewhere.'

What happens if I'm not approved?

In some cases, the panel may feel they need more information before they can reach a decision – this does not mean you have been declined, but it can mean delays, frustration and worry for you. It is done with the best of intentions, though.

For the sake of the child you may be matched with, the panel must be sure of their decision. Your social worker will talk you through this and the possible timescales, should it happen.

Sadly, in some cases the panel declines applications.

The decision maker will send you a letter and should make the reasons for declining you clear. The letter should also explain that you can appeal the decision.

Appealing the decision

Since April 2004, all applicants in England have had the right to appeal the agency's decision.

If you have been declined and you feel you cannot accept this decision, you have 28 days from receiving the agency's letter to appeal.

- You can appeal through your agency's own appeals process or

- You can appeal through the Independent Review Mechanism (IRM).

The IRM is run by the British Association for Adoption and Fostering (BAAF) on behalf of the government's Department for Children, Schools and Families (DCSF).

The IRM cannot make the decision maker overturn their decision, but the IRM will submit their findings to the agency, and the decision maker must take these into account when reconsidering your application.

The IRM isn't there to help if you wish to complain about your agency, however. If you feel you have been mistreated, this must happen through your agency's own complaints procedure.

For more information on the IRM, visit www.irm-adoption.org.uk.

Summing Up

Your application will be put to a panel of experienced people to consider. Among them will be social workers, agency staff, a medical expert, plus a possible mix of foster carers, adoptive parents, adult adoptees and professionals like teachers.

They may wish to ask for further information on a number of points and you will be invited to attend the panel and answer these yourself. Your social worker may also answer questions about your application.

The panel will seem very daunting and powerful, but they only want to ensure every adopter approved is appropriate and will cope with any child placed with them. In short, they need to put the potential child's needs first.

The panel will make their recommendation to the agency's decision maker, who will let you know the final decision by letter.

If you are declined and feel you cannot accept this, you can appeal directly to the agency or through the IRM.

Chapter Seven

Matching and Making it Official

Finding children

Once you have been approved to adopt, the next step is to be matched with a child.

You may feel powerless and a bit deflated waiting for a call from your social worker. In fact, as well as your social worker looking for potential matches for you, there are a number of ways that you can get involved with the search.

It can take within a matter of weeks and months or, in some cases, over a year to find a suitable match. However, adopters who are able to meet the needs of an older child, a group of siblings or a child with complicated needs, may be matched far quicker.

'It can take within a matter of weeks and months or, in some cases, over a year to find a suitable match.'

Magazines

There are two main family-finding magazines in the UK. Children are featured, along with contact details for their social workers so interested prospective adopters can call for more information.

The UK charity, Adoption UK, publish the monthly family-finding magazine *Children Who Wait*, which is available to members of the charity. Each issue contains information on around 100 children who are looking for forever families. There is also an online version available to subscribers to the charity.

For more information, visit www.adoptionuk.org or call 01295 752240.

BAAF publish the monthly family-finding magazine, *Be My Parent*, and an online equivalent. Each magazine features between 200 and 300 children's' profiles. You will need to subscribe to the magazine to receive it. For more information, visit www.bemyparent.org.uk or call 020 7421 2666/5/4.

Once you see a child or sibling group that you feel you could parent, there should be a contact number accompanying the profile for you to call.

Adoption register

The Adoption Register is run by BAAF and, in a nutshell, helps to match up approved adopters with children awaiting adoption in England and Wales. Although it probably sounds like a really obvious idea, until the register there was no easy way of matching adopters and children from different agencies. Adoption agencies don't have comprehensive information about all the children and families outside their own region.

The register's computerised database contains details of children who are awaiting adoption and have not been found suitable families from their own area. Similarly, the database has listings of approved adopters who have not been matched with suitable children by their own agency.

- 109 children were matched between 1 December 2004 and 30 November 2005.

- 157 children were matched between 1 December 2005 and 30 November 2006.

- 199 children were matched between 1 December 2006 and 30 November 2007.

- 41 children were matched between 1 December 2007 and 29 February 2008.

Statistics from The Adoption Register, March 2008.

There are humans at the heart of the register and a team of trained operators and family placement social workers look through information to see if they can spot potential matches between the two groups.

The register works with adoption agencies (and consortia of agencies) to try and improve the chances of a forever family for waiting children.

How successful is the register?

So far, 506 children have been matched at panel with families through the Adoption Register since December 2004.

Agency consortia

To help give children the best chance of finding a suitable adoptive family as quickly as possible, some agencies join forces as an agency consortium.

Consortia tend to be grouped by area, in other words neighbouring authorities or VAs pool their resources and share information on adopters and children to try and make matches and create families. Consortia also pool their resources to improve the training and support on offer to adoptive families.

Consortia often specialise in hard-to-place children, for example children with high degrees of disability or special needs or sibling groups.

If you'd like to know more about a consortium in your area or the one your agency belongs to, the first step is to discuss this with your agency social worker.

The child's background

If your social worker has come up with a possible match for you, he or she will get in touch to discuss the child.

It's very difficult not to get excited! The important thing to remember is that the match has to be right, for you and for the child you are matched with, and it's important to explore any doubts or concerns thoroughly.

If you would like to find out more about the child you will be given some written information. This should include health and medical information as well as the background about the birth family situation.

You will also get to meet with the child's social worker and in some cases an adoption medical adviser to discuss any health issues. You should also be able to meet with the child's foster carer.

You will be able to discuss possible support packages, including financial support, which you may need to meet the child's needs.

If everyone agrees to go ahead with the match, then a more formal meeting is arranged between all these parties and the match is presented to the adoption panel to see if they will formally agree to the adoption.

Matching panel

The adoption panel will be made up of a similar set of people that decided on your suitability to adopt. So there'll be social workers, a medical advisor, possibly a county councillor and other people that may include a foster carer, adoptive parents and an adult adoptee. You have the option to attend the panel, but you don't have to as your social worker can answer questions about your application.

The panel will make a recommendation about whether they feel you would be a suitable parent – or parents – to the child. However, it will be down to the agency decision maker – a senior member of staff – to make the ultimate decision and you'll hear about this within around seven days.

Meeting the child – introductions

'Once the adoption panel have agreed to the proposed match, arrangements will be made for you to be introduced to your prospective child.'

Once the adoption panel have agreed to the proposed match, arrangements will be made for you to be introduced to your prospective child. This is an incredibly exciting and nerve-wracking time!

The first time you meet will probably take place in the child's foster home so they are in familiar, comfortable surroundings. After this initial meeting you'll be asked to attend a placement panel meeting.

What happens at a placement panel meeting?

The meeting will be held to draw up a more structured plan for introductions and the future placement. The child's social worker, your social worker, the foster carer and a fostering link worker will also attend the meeting.

This will look at how you will be introduced to the child, any support needed, any contact issues to take into account – where children have an ongoing contact with their birth family – and how you can have parental responsibility during the placement but before the official adoption order is granted.

A draft adoption placement plan will be drawn up and you will get a copy to keep hold of. At the end of introductions (more on these below), you will need to notify the adoption agency in writing if you wish to continue with the placement. The adoption placement plan should have a space in it for you to complete and use as notification.

Introductions

During the introductions you'll be able to get to know your child and they will get to know you. This will start in the foster carer's home and local area and will gradually build up to the child coming to visit your home and local area, when you and the child are more comfortable with each other.

The child's foster carer will be able to give you invaluable insights into the child's life and development during the time they've spent together.

Some things to ask the foster carer:

- Food likes and dislikes.
- Favourite toys, books, activities and television programmes.
- Any phobias.
- Daily routine.
- Weekly activities like football club or story time at the library.

Foster carers will be able to tell you about any significant day-to-day events and should be able to show you photos – don't be afraid to ask to see these!

The introductions will be planned around the individual case and the needs of the child, so it's impossible to give a concrete idea of time. The average is between two and six weeks, but this will depend on the child's age, personality and experience, needs and level of understanding. For a child under one introductions could be every day for a week or fortnight, whereas for an older child they're likely to be more gradual. Your social worker and the child's social worker should support you and be available to you during the introduction period.

Don't be surprised if you end each visit absolutely exhausted. Introductions can be extremely draining both emotionally and physically. This is normal! Try and cut out any unnecessary chores and hassles during this time so you can relax and rest as much as possible.

Will the child have been prepared?

The child's foster carer should have discussed the upcoming changes with the child in an age-appropriate way. The child's social worker should also have done some preparation work with the child.

> 'The child's foster carer will be able to give you invaluable insights into the child's life and development during the time they've spent together.'

Family book

In preparation for placement you will be asked to create a family book or family album. This is your time to get really creative! Some adopters have likened this to the 'baby book' idea that expectant birth parents often draw up, and it can be a very special experience.

You can use pictures, photos, memorabilia and, of course, worded descriptions to introduce your new child to their new home, their new bedroom, any pets, their new school or nursery, their new grandparents or extended family and anything else you want to share with them.

Some ideas for the family book:

- For younger children, a special toy that you intend to give to them can be photographed in a range of rooms and locations that your child will come to know.

- You can use characters like the family dog or cat to introduce pictures and ideas.

- If you have a child or children already, you could make them the 'narrator' of the book.

- Consider how you'd like to refer to yourself or selves – will you use first names, mum, mummy, dad, daddy or something else? It may be worth asking the foster carer or child's social worker which names they think are appropriate.

- Depending on how good you are with sticky tape and sugar paper, you could make little pull out sections with pictures behind doors and windows, a little like an advent calendar.

Placement

When everyone agrees that the time is right for introductions to finish and for the child to move in with you, they will do so on a set date. This date may have already been set during the placement planning meeting or during a review of how the introductions are going.

This period is a little like a cross between introductions and formal adoption. The child will be living as part of the family and you will have limited parental responsibility, plus support from the agency and social workers, but the child will not formally be your child yet.

This is the final stage of legal adoption. The agency has a statutory duty to visit regularly during this time, review how things are going and give you support.

'In preparation for placement you will be asked to create a family book or family album. This is your time to get really creative!'

Parental responsibility

Under the Adoption and Children Act 2002, adoptive parents in England and Wales will have parental responsibility from the date of placement. You will not have sole parental responsibility yet though.

The child's birth parents and the LA placing the child will also retain parental responsibility, which means that other holders of parental responsibility may be able influence certain key decisions such as medical care and schooling. If the authority placing the child plans to limit the extent of your parental responsibility, they must discuss this with you before placement.

Once the adoption is official, you – and your partner if you have one – will have exclusive parental responsibility and the LA and birth parents will not.

Official adoption order

A minimum of 10 weeks must pass before you can apply to a court for an official adoption order. It's important that you're happy to go ahead and feel confident that the child is settled into your home and that you have the support in place to continue.

Once the order is granted, the child is formally yours – all rights and responsibilities move from the agency and onto you.

The agency should be prepared to support this application before you go ahead.

'Once the adoption is official, you will have exclusive parental responsibility, the LA and birth parents will not.'

How much does this cost?

The court fee for an adoption order is currently £140 per child; the standard charge applies at any court to which the application is made.

How do I apply?

In England and Wales an adoption application can be made to any court including Magistrates, the County Courts or the High Court. You don't have to make an application to the same court that granted the care order, freeing order or placement order. In Scotland you need to lodge a petition in the Sheriff Court or the Court of Session. In Northern Ireland you can apply to either the County Court or the High Court.

You will need to request an application form from the court, complete it and return it. The agency that you adopted through should help you with your application. Once the application has been completed the court will require a social worker from the authority that placed your child to complete a thorough report.

In England and Wales this is called an Annex A report. In Scotland it is called a section 22 or 23 report. The report will contain information about the child, their birth family, your family and how the placement has gone so far.

In some cases, the court may appoint an independent person (a child's guardian in England and Wales; a curator ad litem in Scotland) to prepare a report and they will talk to you and the child's birth parents.

Your day in court

If the birth parents have agreed to the adoption, hearings tend to be short and straightforward – usually under half an hour, with the order granted at the time.

You, and older children, may be asked some questions if necessary. The judge will need to consider the feelings of the child and take age and level of understanding into account.

Many adoptive families make a special day out of this; if you feel it's right for you and your children, go for it!

A good judge will make a fuss of the children and keep the day light-hearted and friendly. Courts can be daunting places for children and a friendly judge can make all the difference – unfortunately this is something out of your control.

You may wish to bring a couple of supportive members of your family too and make a day of it with a special lunch or tea afterwards.

Contested adoption

Birth parents can contest an adoption right up until the adoption order is granted. This sounds terrifying, but it does not mean the adoption will not go ahead.

Many times any potential chance of consent not being given will have been considered by the court before the child has been placed for adoption, in some circumstances the court will outright over-ride the wishes of the birth parents.

A child's guardian (England/Wales), curator ad litem (Scotland) or guardian ad litem (Northern Ireland) is appointed by the court to investigate and advise the court on the child's best interests.

Don't panic; a contested adoption does not mean that you will not be able to formally adopt the child that you have had placed with you, it simply means the birth parents are exercising their right to make their feelings known.

Summing Up

This is one of the most gruelling parts of the process. You go from being hopeful prospective adopters to parents, via placement and a court case. You'd be forgiven for being terrified!

The most important thing is getting support – from your social worker, your agency, your friends and your family. Don't take this all on your own head: talk about it, write down your thoughts, try and get some rest and relaxation – even if this is 10 minutes reading time before sleep.

You will be introduced to your child carefully, and they – and you – should have had help preparing for the changes ahead.

Your child will then come to stay with you, for at least 10 months before you can apply for an official adoption order.

Chapter Eight

Life Story Work

Life story work is a tool to record information about a child's early life. The research is carried out by the child's social worker, in preparation for adoption, but the actual work tends to be done by the child's foster carer or resident social worker.

Children who have been separated from their birth families may not remember much of their early years or of key figures and experiences. They may even have blocked out chunks of memory as part of a coping strategy or due to injury.

Why is this needed?

Life story work helps apply a timeline and an order to disrupted experiences and often multiple homes with multiple figures. It can give children a way to explore their memories, questions about their birth families, and create a valuable record of photographs, drawings and information.

The process of life story work can help children come to terms with their early experiences and build a sense of who they are and how they fit into the world.

What should be covered?

It really depends on the child, their age, experiences and willingness to be involved.

Life story work will try to help children answer these questions:

- Who am I?
- How did I get here?
- Where am I going?

'Children who have been separated from their birth families may not remember much of their early years or of key figures and experiences.'

Good life story work will start by exploring what the child remembers from their early life and any questions they may have. Some children will have a very clear, chronological idea of the circumstances surrounding them leaving their birth family – but many will not. Life story work will attempt to remedy that.

Ethnic, cultural and religious background is also important as life story work can be a chance for a child to explore their birth family's roots and origins.

The information should then form a life story book.

Should the children help?

Yes, absolutely. Life story work is for them, predominantly, though the feelings and issues that it brings to the surface are invaluable in helping you to understand your child and their feelings.

Children won't always be immediately receptive to life story work and it must be handled gently and introduced gradually.

Photographs and information

It's the responsibility of the child's social worker to gather information and ideally photographs to form part of the life story book.

It depends on individual circumstances but the social worker will try and seek information and photographs from birth parents, grandparents, siblings, wider family, school or nursery staff, friends and medical records.

When your child first became looked after, their birth certificate, photographs and special keepsakes may have been gathered in preparation, but this is not always the case.

Summing Up

Life story work is an incredibly valuable tool for helping children make sense of the fractured memories and experiences of their early lives.

The process can throw up discussions and realisations that may not have been uncovered otherwise. These can help you to better understand your child and for them to better understand themselves.

The life story book that is developed through this work will be something for you and your child to keep forever, and you can continue the work throughout their childhood.

Chapter Nine

Your Shopping List and First Days at Home

Introducing children to other family members

Firstly, don't be bullied!

Your friends and family may well want to come and welcome your child into the wider family at the earliest opportunity – yet, however compelling their arguments, you must stand your ground! You are now this child's parent and you have every right to ask for some space.

You and your child have been through an incredible process of change and your child has already met the most important new face – yours! It's in no-one's best interests to then bamboozle them with more new faces, names and personalities.

Explain to your loved ones, gently, that you're thrilled by the reception and interest, but that you've got to be very careful in how you introduce people and must do everything very gently.

Advice for new grandparents, aunts and uncles

It is very important that grandparents, aunts and uncles respect the new family's space and the need to bond and settle.

As exciting as it can be, the child will have had a huge period of adjustment and will be experiencing confusion and feelings of loss. Introducing too many new faces at once will only add to this anxiety.

'You are now this child's parent and you have every right to ask for some space.'

Your time will come, but it must be left to the adoptive parents to introduce family members on their terms.

Getting organised

Babies and toddlers – your shopping list

- Safety equipment including stair gates, socket covers, baby monitors, room thermometers and toddler reins for walking.

- A cot or cot bed and bedding – never a duvet for under-ones though.

- Plenty of bodysuits and vests – you can never have too many of these!

- A jacket, hat and mittens.

- A baby bath or bath-seat.

- Nappies, baby wipes, bubble bath and baby shampoo – it's worth buying the same brands as the foster carer as familiar smells help with the settling-in process.

- A pushchair, which should be able to lie flat for very new babies.

Three to five-year-olds – your shopping list

- Depending on age and needs, you may need a lightweight stroller for longer journeys.

- A Potty.

- A car seat.

- Bed and bedding, which can be a lightweight duvet.

- Children's cutlery, crockery and beakers.

- Kids' shampoo and body wash.

- A step for reaching the basin.

- Flannels and sponges

Six-years plus – your shopping list

- Bed and bedding.
- Other bedroom furniture.
- Booster car seat.
- Crockery and beakers.
- A good selection of age-appropriate books.
- Kids' shampoo and body wash.
- School equipment and stationery.

Try to leave as much as possible for your child to pick with you

Older children – your shopping list

- Bed and bedding.
- Other bedroom furniture.
- Toiletries.
- School equipment and stationery.

Try to leave as much as possible for your child to pick with you.

Depending on your child's physical needs and challenges, there may be additional disability-specific equipment that is needed and your social worker – and child's social worker – must help you devise a full list.

Summing Up

The first days with your new child will be head-spinning, exciting, terrifying, exhausting, thrilling and a million other emotions!

Don't be surprised if you go from exhilarating highs to extreme lows. Not many people admit it openly, but you wouldn't be the first new adopter to cry your eyes out in despair and fear once your new child is sleeping upstairs for the first time.

You are on the precipice of a whole new life. A wonderful life, but one with challenges, sleepless nights and huge changes to your lifestyle. You have every right to be shattered and bewildered.

Take a deep breathe, run a hot bath, have a glass of wine and try and get some sleep. Don't beat yourself up for how you feel, even if your reaction has taken you by surprise.

Your friends and family may well want to race in and meet your new child and shower them with gifts and cuddles. It's lovely, but it's not always appropriate and you have every right to ask them to take a step back and take things slowly.

You may want to go on a huge shopping spree and have a room stuffed with toys and new clothes for your child. Obviously you need to get some essentials and it's important that a room is child-friendly and comfortable, but picking some new bits and pieces with your child is a wonderful way to get to know them and their likes and dislikes, so try not to go too mad in advance!

'The first days with your new child will be head-spinning, exciting, terrifying, exhausting, thrilling and a million other emotions!'

Chapter Ten

Contact with Birth Family

Before the adoption order is made, the court will consider whether any arrangements for contact with birth relatives would be in the best interests of your child.

Your views, the opinions and hopes of the birth family and the professional opinions of the social workers involved in the case will be taken into consideration, but of course it is your child's interests that are the priority.

You will not be under legal obligation to stick to any contact that's recommended, but it is advisable. Each case is different and there are various different options that will be considered.

Meeting birth parents

Scary, eh? A vision of confrontation and raw emotion is likely to strike fear in the heart of any prospective adopter. Overwhelmingly though, tough as this is, meeting your child's birth mother or father is a unique opportunity.

Having a picture of you with your child's birth mother or father can be a source of comfort and interest to your child later on in their life – you may feel this is inappropriate given poor or abusive care, however.

There is a real chance to show that, while it must have been an incredibly tough experience for the birth parent, their agreement to meet shows a level of acceptance for what has happened and the new family set-up.

By meeting the birth parents you will see facial features and expressions which you may see in your own little one and you can ask questions about your child's early days if you feel comfortable.

'Overwhelmingly though, tough as this is, meeting your child's birth mother or father is a unique opportunity.'

Meeting foster families

The foster carer who has looked after your child can tell you invaluable secrets about your little one: their likes and dislikes, favourite stories, phobias, anxieties. They can tell you tiny nuggets of information that can make all the difference: what soap powder to use so the smell is familiar, what bubble bath they love, what song always sends them to sleep and so on.

You might worry that your child's foster carer will give you a hard time or interrogate you, but the reality is likely to be very different. You – and not the foster carer – have been approved to adopt your child and the foster carer will respect this. They may feel terribly sad about saying goodbye, but as a foster carer they will be resigned to this.

Foster carers will often have worked wonders with children, giving them a sense of structure and routine, family and comfort. You should have met your child's foster carer several times during introductions.

Letterbox contact

The most common form of contact by far, letterbox contact enables birth relatives to send letters, gifts and photos to children via a third party address managed by the authority/agency that placed your child with you. Adopters and adoptees can then send letters and photos back if this feels appropriate and comfortable.

By using the letterbox service, identities and addresses are protected and contact can be controlled and occasional.

Direct contact

Direct contact with birth parents is rare, however direct contact with birth siblings and other relatives can be a very happy and enriching experience for your child. Every situation is different though and your social worker and your child's social worker can talk through the implications of this.

It's understandable to be nervous about this, after all this will be your child, and by having them spending time with their 'old' family, won't this undermine your new family? The answer is, no, it's not that simple.

The fact is, your child does not forget their past the minute they arrive in your home, nor would it be healthy for them to. Their past has happened and maintaining links can help your child feel secure and at ease with their situation.

There are many situations where direct contact with a birth parent is not appropriate – particularly when there has been abuse or physical threat. But it may be that direct contact with siblings and extended family is deemed a good idea.

Direct contact should never be sprung on you though; this should have been discussed during the matching stage and built into the placement plan. You should have a chance to discuss this with your social worker and receive ongoing support from your agency.

Summing Up

Every case is different and there are many ways for your child to maintain some link to their past and their birth relatives.

Maintaining contact in a safe and secure way can help to consolidate your child's ideas about their early life, their place in the world and the way the several stages of their life fit together.

Ultimately, while your child is your dependant, you can veto contact if you feel it is having a negative effect. The courts have the power to make orders for contact, but only if adoptive parents are in agreement. However, they can make orders for sibling contact even when adoptive parents are opposed to this.

Chapter Eleven

Education

Arranging school places

If your child is of school age or is due to turn five in the next school year, you will need to arrange a school place for him or her.

If your child has already been in education, you may have an idea (either from the child's social worker or the foster carer) about how they view school, how they have performed academically and any special educational needs.

If your child is already of school age, you can contact local schools directly to find out about spaces. Try and visit any potential schools and meet the teaching staff and office staff. Visiting within school hours will give you a better understanding of the atmosphere.

Every child of school age (five to 16) is entitled to a place at a state school – but this doesn't mean they will automatically get a place at your preferred school. This tends to be because many schools get more applications than they have places to offer and schools have the right to limit the number of admissions they accept for the year. You may be offered a place on the waiting list, however.

If your child is under five and due to start school in the next September, contact your LA to find out if you need to apply directly to the school or via the council.

Giving background history to school

Your child's story, in one sense, is theirs to tell. But on a practical level, the experiences your child has been through will affect how they react, not just to authority or structure or a new school, but to more day-to-day things such as lesson topics.

Themed learning, for example, often involves the self or the family. Children may be asked to bring in baby photos or talk about family trees. This can be confusing at best, through to deeply traumatic.

So there is a practical purpose to giving teaching staff an overview of your child's background and any triggers to avoid.

Dealing with problems

Teachers have recently been given guidelines on avoiding assumptions about pupils' home lives. In theory, teachers shouldn't suggest that a pupil lives with a birth mum and a birth dad.

If you feel like a teacher has overstepped the mark or has handled a situation incorrectly and you don't feel you can raise it directly with them, try and speak to your child's head of year or one of the more senior staff.

You don't have to go in all gun's blazing, especially if you don't feel comfortable with this approach, but do try and organise your thoughts and record your reasons, perhaps jotted in a diary so that you have a record of any concerns and a way to structure your argument.

Home-schooling

In the words of the charity Education Otherwise, 'education is compulsory, schooling is not'.

Parents in England and Wales legally have to ensure that children of school age (five to 16) receive an effective education. In the majority of cases, this means ensuring their children attend school on a regular basis, but this responsibility can be met in the home.

The responsibility of parents is clearly established in section 7 of the Education Act 1996 (previously section 36 of the Education Act 1944), which says:

'The parent of every child of compulsory school age shall cause him to receive efficient full-time education suitable

a) to his age, ability and aptitude, and

b) to any special educational needs he may have, either by regular attendance at school or otherwise.'

If you feel your child's experiences at school are unsafe, unsettled, unhappy or counter-productive, you don't have to stick with the standard programme and put them into your local school full-time.

Home-schooling is a controversial area, one that many people – with experience or not – seem to have opinions on, yet every child's educational needs are different and with all the will in the world a blanket approach to lessons and a group experience simply does not always work.

Considerations

- Schooling your child puts an enormous pressure on your time and your relationship; what respite could you consider? Could you send your child to a local school for part of the curriculum? Will a member of your support network be able to take your child out a couple of times a week and give you both a break from each other?

- How will you ensure your child remains socialised and does not become reclusive or uneasy in group situations?

- Do you feel equipped to effectively teach your child a broad curriculum? Are there areas of the curriculum you could improve upon through your own learning?

- How will you structure the learning? Will you aim for a child-led, explorative experience or a highly structured system of lessons and learning similar to that of a traditional school? Or perhaps somewhere in between?

Child Benefit

Providing your child was being home-educated before they turned 16, you can continue to claim Child Benefit for them while they are being educated after the age of 16 (currently up to the age of 19).

For more information

UK Charity, Education Otherwise, is a membership organisation that provides information and support for families with children being educated outside traditional schooling.

For more information, visit www.education-otherwise.org.

Specialist schools

Space in specialist and therapeutic schools is a rare commodity, and sadly the number of applications outweighs the number of school spaces. However, your child may benefit from help and support that a mainstream school cannot provide.

Some specialist schools focus on a particular subject area such as creative arts, music or sport. Alongside this focus they still follow the national curriculum.

To find a list of specialist schools in your area, your first point of call should be your LA.

Independent schools

Independent private schools in England, Wales and Scotland tend to have smaller class sizes and a higher ratio of staff to pupils than state schools. They are also allowed to set their own curriculum.

There are over 2,000 independent schools in England alone and these are funded through fees paid by parents, income from investments and – in over half of all cases – charitable donations.

Independent schools have their own admissions process and criteria so you will need to speak to each individual school that you may be interested in.

Although they are free to set their own curriculum and admissions process, all independent schools need to register with the Department for Children, Schools and Families and will be monitored regularly either by Ofsted or the Independent Schools Inspectorate.

Residential schools

Some independent private schools are residential, while some specialist therapeutic schools offer residential places. These will often specialise in a spectrum of similar or related challenges, such as Asperger's syndrome or ADHD.

Specialist therapeutic schools tend to be heavily over-subscribed and reliant on charity status.

Summing Up

While the majority of children in the UK are educated within a state school, this is not the only form of education available and may not always be the right one for your family.

It's important to research all the options available to you locally and nationally. Finances are obviously a consideration and you may need to approach your adoption agency for a support package.

You may find that the first school you enrol your child in may not be able to cater for their needs as well as you hoped, so be prepared to be flexible and open-minded to change.

For more information in these areas, see *Working Mothers – The Essential Guide* and *Special Educational Needs – A Parent's Guide.*

Chapter Twelve
Benefits and Family Finances

Budget preparation

You're bound to have thought long and hard about your household finances and how you'll manage when a child is placed with you.

When you're in the process of your home study, your social worker is likely to talk to you about any savings and outgoings you have and how you will manage if the family income is reduced as a result of one or both adopters giving up work or reducing work hours.

There may be allowances available – either on placement or ongoing – but this is not guaranteed.

Adoption leave

If you are employed and you adopt a child, you may be entitled to 52 weeks of adoption leave. Only one member of a couple can take paid leave, so if you are both entitled to it you will need to choose which one of you will take the paid leave.

The other employed member of the couple could be entitled to paternity pay, though.

Paternity leave

If you wish to apply for paternity leave, you must have been employed continuously by your current employer for 26 weeks or more.

According to the Trade Union Congress (TUC), you are entitled to take either one week or two consecutive weeks' paternity leave. The time when you can take paternity leave will start from the day your adopted child is placed with you and will finish 56 days after that date. You can start your leave on the day of placement or a set number of days after placement, or a set date that you have specified to your employer.

Statutory Adoption Pay

New rights to Statutory Adoption Pay and Leave and Statutory Paternity Pay and Leave came into force in England, Scotland and Wales in April 2003. The pay structures apply to couples and single people who are adopting within the UK.

How much?

2008–2009 Statutory Adoption Pay (SAP) is paid for a maximum of 26 weeks at a rate of either £106 a week or 90% of your weekly earnings – whichever figure is lower.

2008–2009 Statutory Paternity Pay (SPP) is paid for a maximum of two weeks at a rate of either £108.85 a week or 90% of your average weekly earnings – whichever figure is lower.

SAP and SPP in Northern Ireland

In December 2002, new rights to SAP and SPP came into force. As with the rest of the UK, they apply to couples or single people adopting a child in the UK.

How much?

2008–2009 Statutory Adoption Pay (SAP) is paid for a maximum of 26 weeks at a rate of either £102.80 a week or 90% of your weekly earnings – whichever figure is lower.

2008–2009 Statutory Paternity Pay (SPP) is paid for a maximum of two weeks at a rate of either £102.80 a week or 90% of your average weekly earnings – whichever figure is lower.

Adoption Allowance

Since 1991, adoption agencies have been able to pay adoption allowances in some circumstances. In 2003, the regulations were tightened up in light of the new rules governing support for adopters.

Adoption Allowance isn't a standard right to all adopters though. It's more of a safety net – an allowance paid where an adoption wouldn't be able to continue or wouldn't be practical to continue without additional financial help. The money could be to cover additional costs of caring for a large sibling group or a child's special needs.

Who can get it?

In England, there are set circumstances where financial support may be considered. These are laid down in The Adoption Support Services Regulations 2005:

- Where it is essential to make sure the adopter(s) can continue to care for the child.

- Where the child has a need for special care due to an illness, disability, emotional or behavioural difficulties or the effect of past abuse or neglect

- Where the LA needs to make special arrangements to make sure the placement or adoption goes ahead because of:

    - The age or ethnic background of the child.

- The need to place the child with the same adoptive parent(s) as his or her sibling(s).

- Where financial support is needed to cover the cost of travel for direct contact with a birth relative.

- Where the LA believes it's appropriate to contribute to the cost of:

  - Legal fees including court fees for an adoption.

  - Expenses necessary during introductions.

  - Expenses for accommodating and looking after the child including furniture, transport, toys, home adaptations etc.

The full specifications are laid down in The Adoption Support Services Regulations 2005.

Scotland

Adoption allowances are available in Scotland. For full details on the procedure for determining who is eligible and for how much, see the Adoption Allowance Regulations 1996 (Statutory Instrument 1996 No. 3257 (S.247)).

For more information, visit www.hmso.gov.uk.

Northern Ireland

Adoption allowances are available in Northern Ireland. For full details on the procedure for determining who is eligible and for how much, see the Adoption Allowance Regulations (Northern Ireland) 1996 (Statutory Rule 1996 No. 438).

For more information, visit www.hmso.gov.uk.

Child Benefit

Child Benefit is a tax-free, four-weekly payment, which is not means-tested and can be claimed by anyone bringing up children up to the age of 16 (or 19 if in full-time education).

For 2008–2009, the rate of Child Benefit is:

- £18.80 per week for the eldest or only child.

- £12.55 per week for each other child.

You can apply for Child Benefit from the day your child is placed with you. You will need to apply (either online or by post) and will need to give HM Revenue & Customs some key information, such as details of the agency you have adopted through, a named social worker (who will need to confirm the date your child was placed) and your child's date of birth.

You may be asked to confirm this information again – sadly, it isn't always a quick and easy process!

Tax credits

Tax credits are simply payments from the government to help with everyday costs. The two tax credits that you may be able to claim when a child is placed are Child Tax Credit and Working Tax Credit.

According to the HM Revenue & Customs, nine out of 10 families with children are entitled to tax credits. The HMRC website (www.hmrc.gov.uk) has a handy calculator for working out if you are entitled to help.

You may claim tax credits if you are fostering or have adopted a child who has been placed with you by a LA, providing:

- The child was being looked after by the LA and then fostered with you and

- The cost of the child's accommodation or maintenance is not being met in part or full out of LA funds or public funds.

OR

- The child was not being looked after by an LA but was placed for adoption by them and

- The LA is not making a payment for the child's accommodation or maintenance.

Rate of Working Tax Credit £ per year (2008–2009)

Rates and Thresholds	£ per year
Basic element	£1,800
Couple and lone parent element	£1,770
30-hour working a week element	£735
Disabled worker element	£2,405
Severe disability element	£1,020
50+ Return to work payment (16-29 hours)	£1,235
50+ Return to work payment (30+ hours)	£1,840

Childcare element of the Working Tax Credit £ per week (2008–2009)

Rates and Thresholds	£ per week
Maximum eligible cost for one child	£175
Maximum eligible cost for two or more children	£300
Percentage of eligible costs covered	80%

Rate of Child Tax Credit £ per year (2008–2009)

Rates and Thresholds	£ per year
Child Tax Credit Family element	£545
Family element, baby addition	£545
Child element	£2,085
Disabled child element	£2,540
Severely disabled child element	£1,020

(All information sourced from HM Revenue & Customs)

Housing Benefit and Council Tax Benefit

- Housing Benefit is paid by local councils to help with the cost of rent.

- Council Tax Benefit is paid by local councils to cover part or all of your council tax bill.

Both benefits are paid for those on a low income. Council Tax Benefit is payable to those who rent and homeowners, however Housing Benefit is purely for those who rent their home – either privately or through a housing association.

Savings of £6,000 or more will affect the amount of Housing Benefit you can receive.

Summing Up

Although you will have looked at your income and outgoings before starting the adoption process, there are various benefits, allowances and credits that you can apply for once you have a child placed with you.

There are various sources of additional money and it can take some time to go through and apply for each.

If you have access to the internet, you will find the HM Revenue & Customs website (www.hmrc.gov.uk) is very useful as a starting point. Another handy website is www.entitledto.co.uk, which can give you an idea of all the standard benefits and tax credits your family may be able to claim.

If possible, it is a good idea to put some money aside in advance of placement as money from benefits and credits can take a while to come through. The less you have to worry about during the first few weeks of placement the better!

'There are various sources of additional money and it can take some time to go through and apply for each.'

Chapter Thirteen

Attachment Disorder and Problems

What problems may occur?

No child enters an adoption without some form of trauma in their past. This may sound stark, but by definition adoption follows family break-down. Ignoring anything else the child may have gone through, this upheaval alone is traumatic.

Adopted children often suffer medical conditions as a result of their early care, maternal drug use during pregnancy or genetic predisposition. Consequently, it's important to find out as much as possible about any known conditions (physical, mental or emotional) but also how much investigation has been done. The more you know at the matching stage, the earlier you can start to address your child's needs and ensure that their life with you is as happy and comfortable as possible.

Some issues may not have been detected at birth or during the early years, so it's important to have an open mind about what may present itself further down the line. Knowing as much as possible about the birth family, your child's early experiences and homes can help, and please never be afraid to press your agency for as much information as possible!

'Adopted children often suffer medical conditions as a result of their early care, maternal drug use during pregnancy or genetic predisposition.'

Attachment Disorder

It's impossible to fully cover Attachment Disorder in under a chapter, and I strongly suggest you read more on it so that you are armed with information.

It's not tempting fate, or being a doomsayer, but the sad truth is Attachment Disorder can be a difficult by-product of adoption and the sooner you are able to work with your child, your wider family and professionals like teachers, the sooner you can help your child.

In many cases, adopted children will not have experienced safe, healthy attachments in their early years. Simple things like getting picked up when they cried as babies may never have happened.

The attachment that forms between a parent and a child is usually an instinctive and natural thing. It helps a child develop emotions, boundaries and ways to communicate.

When that bond and experience has been disrupted in some way, either through neglect, abuse or loss, the child's development will have been affected and problems may be displayed through challenging and upsetting behaviour.

A secure attachment means that a child doesn't want a parent to leave and is comforted by their return. With Attachment Disorder, this simple equation breaks down in a number of ways.

Avoidant Attachment: A child shows no distress at the parent leaving or a tangible response when the parent returns.

Ambivalent Attachment: This is a very confusing form of attachment and can be easily missed. A child shows distress when the parent leaves but is willing to be comforted by a stranger, then shows a reluctance to warm to the returning parent.

Disorganised Attachment: A child experiencing a disorganised attachment will struggle to adapt to a parent's return and may start to freeze or rock.

Children suffering with Attachment Disorder will often display similar symptoms to those attributed to ADHD, so do take amateur diagnoses of ADHD (or indeed, anything else) with a pinch of salt!

Attachment disordered children can present angry and threatening behaviour, often avoiding intimacy and close relationships, or switching between menacing, paranoid and charming.

This is not an exhaustive list by any means, but common symptoms of the disorder include:

- Problems in social situations such as avoiding eye contact; difficulty with making friends; controlling behaviour and babbling.

- Emotional problems like lack of empathy; affection with strangers; demanding, clingy behaviour; difficulty with articulating feelings; resentment; jealousy; angry outbursts and severe, long-winded tantrums.

- Behavioural problems such as anger and aggression aimed at carers – especially mothers. Problems include self-sabotaging or confrontational behaviour; refusal to accept any blame; inability to control impulses; sexual acting out; stealing, lying or blaming new parents for the actions of birth families or past abusers; breaking possessions and hurting animals.

- Developmental problems can include poor awareness of danger or cause and effect; food issues such as hoarding or gorging; confused morals and conscience; self-neglect and poor hygiene.

Mental health

No child comes into the adoption system without experiencing some form of trauma. This in itself can cause psychiatric issues that may need some working through, either as a family or with a therapist.

Experts argue about the extent to which adoption can itself 'cause' mental health issues, and it's very hard to find a definitive answer when so many different factors can affect current and future issues.

As with physical challenges, the early life of an adopted child that experiences inconsistent care, neglect, drug use or inherited problems can be factors in mental health concerns.

'The attachment that forms between a parent and a child is usually an instinctive and natural thing.'

In preparation for adoption, any known or found mental health issues should have been disclosed to you but don't be afraid to ask if this isn't the case – you are entitled to ask to see your child's medical reports. If a paediatrician has been involved in the case, you can also ask to meet with him or her to ask for more information.

Before matching, you can ask your social worker to find out as much as possible about any mental health issues known to run in the birth family. None of this is a guarantee for the future but any information you can gather can help you to prepare.

Physical health

Many children within the care system have disabilities or special physical needs. In some cases these were present before and at birth, but some may be hereditary, some may have presented in later childhood and some may be the direct result of physical abuse or neglect.

Foetal Alcohol Syndrome and children who are suffering from the effects of drug use in utero are over-represented in the system.

There is no book big enough to list and detail every potential physical challenge that may be exhibited by a child in need of adoption, or any child for that matter. The fact is, as much as possible should be discovered during the adoption process through medical history and examination; beyond this there is no way of knowing for sure what the future holds – knowing this and being prepared to adapt is your best strategy for the future.

Birthdays and key dates

Children, especially older children, will have days and experiences that trigger painful memories. In particular, family occasions are a common trigger for confusion and difficulty. The obvious ones – Christmas and birthdays – can be anticipated but there will always be surprises.

'Children, especially older children, will have days and experiences that trigger painful memories. In particular, family occasions are a common trigger for confusion and difficulty.'

You will know your child best. You will know whether cuddles, space or talk is likely to help. Sometimes it will just be a case of seeing what helps. Sometimes nothing helps and you, as a family, just need to ride the tough days out. Sadly, there is no magic formula.

During the introductions you can ask your child's foster carer about any triggers and dates to be aware of, and some hints may be generated through life story work.

Getting some advice and support through the difficult periods is essential and, as patterns form and you start to build up an unwritten calendar of tough times, you can seek support from teachers or childcare workers too.

Summing Up

Thinking about potential problems can leave a bitter taste when you're trying to focus on such an exciting development in your life.

Every child is different, every parent is different and every family is different. It's impossible to know exactly what the future will hold and if you did – well, how boring! But being prepared and knowing that there are people and options to call on if you need them can help you feel calm in the present.

By its very nature, adoption causes feelings of loss, disruption and uncertainty – not just for your child but for you also. For this reason alone, it's important to know that seeking help is a strong and helpful decision for all of you.

'It's impossible to know exactly what the future will hold and if you did – well, how boring!'

From the moment a specific child or sibling group is mentioned to you, you will be forced to consider what you can and can't envisage coping with. Make sure you ask for as much information as possible and don't be shy about grilling absolutely everyone who has cared for your child and investigated their background.

Information is power and your child will be all the better for an informed and prepared mum or dad.

Chapter Fourteen

Post-Adoption Support

Since 31 October 2003 all adoptive families in England and Wales have had the right to request that their LA assesses their needs for adoption support services.

What this really means is that you can demand your LA to look at whether you need help and support (be it financial or professional) and that they cannot ignore you if you ask for help.

This doesn't automatically mean they will agree to give you this help, but they must consider your views and take you seriously. If they decide your family does need access to support services, a plan will be drawn up outlining how the LA will provide these services, via what means and when.

Negotiating a support package

From the moment a specific child or sibling group is mentioned, you need to be strong and ask your social worker to get as much information together as possible.

Health and medical problems and concerns will obviously have a real impact on costs to your family, but emotional, mental and therapeutic needs also have associated costs – sometimes very high ones.

Be very honest with yourself – and your social worker – about any concerns. It may sound cynical, but the placing agency is unlikely to bend over backwards to spell out how serious problems may be. You may need to pin them down to some actual answers, as without a robust support package in place you could end up fighting for desperately needed funds once the placement is under way.

'Be very honest with yourself – and your social worker – about any concerns.'

Don't be superstitious – anticipating possible challenges is not a self-fulfilling prophecy!

The more support you can have waiting for you to tap into should you need it, the less of a draining battle you will have should challenges arise.

Where to go for help

In the first instance, approach your LA. As just explained, they do have a duty to consider what services you may need, although you may then find more help from other organisations.

Post-adoption support in the UK varies wildly from area to area, but most agencies now have an appointed post-adoption worker who you can stay in touch with and use as the first port of call to talk over any issues.

'It sounds obvious, but it really cannot be stressed enough: take time to look after yourself!'

They may also organise training and group support for adopters in the area, as well as giving you information about specialist services that your family may need to access.

In England, the Adoption Support Services Regulations specify that adopters have the right to request and receive an assessment of their post-adoption support needs – including financial support – up until the child is an adult. For the first three years after adoption this responsibility is that of the authority which placed your child, but after the three years it is the responsibility of whichever LA you live within.

Self-care

It sounds obvious, but it really cannot be stressed enough: take time to look after yourself! Whether you are single or in a partnership, you must look after your own well-being before you can be the best possible parent. At times of stress remember what they tell you on aeroplanes: affix your own oxygen mask before your child's.

It need not be so grand as a holiday or even a night out – especially if you are living with a child who needs round-the-clock care – but time out to read, a massage, a 10-minute yoga workout… it all helps to reinvigorate you.

Your support network

You will have discussed your support network right at the start of your adoption journey, well now is the time to call on them!

Some people will surprise you – those you thought would be pillars of support through anything life throws may shrink away, while those you thought would prove to be fair-weather friends can end up transforming your life. Be open to help from wherever you can get it!

Remember that everybody involved in your child's life is technically part of your support network. Your child's teacher, doctor, health visitor and other professionals all know your child and have a viewpoint on them; sometimes this may jar with your experience and opinions, but it can be invaluable.

Further information and organisations

As well as state-funded support, there are organisations and therapists out there that specialise in support and help for adoptive families.

The Post Adoption Centre (PAC) in London is incredibly over-subscribed and very highly regarded. To give you some idea, in 2004 PAC supported 1,850 individuals and families affected by adoption.

PAC helps adoptive families through telephone advice, counselling, child and family therapeutic services, mediation services and more.

Adoption UK is a membership charity that was set up by adopters to help other adoptive families. As well as the family-finding magazine, *Children Who Wait*, the charity provides its members with a helpline, local support groups, access to training courses, information, contact networks and more.

Since 2003, the charity has also run an award-winning online community (www. adoptionuk.org), which enables adopters, prospective adopters and foster carers to support each other 24 hours a day, seven days a week.

Summing Up

Adopting children is a wonderful experience but it can be very challenging and it's vital that you know what support is out there and how to access it.

Your LA should be your first port of call, as legally they have a duty to consider what support services you, as an adoptive family, need access to.

As much as provisions should be in place through a support package negotiated before placement, you may need additional help and support. There are charities and organisations out there that can provide support for adoptive families.

In times of difficulty and challenge, the old adage about knowing who your friends are really comes into play. Ask for help, ask for support, ask them to help you finish a bottle of wine. Let your hair down and look after yourself too.

Help List

For adopters and potential adopters

Adoption Register

Adoption Register Manager, Adoption Register for England & Wales,
Unit 4, Pavilion Business Park, Royds Hall Road, Wortley, Leeds, LS12 6AJ
Tel: 0870 750 2173
mail@adoptionregister.org.uk
www.adoptionregister.org.uk
Adoption agencies do not have detailed information about all the children
and families outside their own region, so the Adoption Register will work with
adoption agencies and adoption consortia to make sure that all children and
families have the best chance of finding a suitable match.

Adoption UK

46 The Green, South Bar Street, Banbury, OX16 9AB
Tel: 01295 752240
www.adoptionuk.org
Adoption UK helps to make adoptions work and promotes loving and
supportive relationships between children and their adoptive families. It
provides independent support, information and advice on good practice to all
concerned with adoption.

British Association of Adoption & Fostering (BAAF)

Saffron House, 6-10 Kirby Street, London, EC1N 8TS
Tel: 020 7421 2600
mail@baaf.org.uk
www.baaf.org.uk

BAAF work with everyone involved with adoption and fostering across the UK. They have regional and country offices in England, Wales, Scotland and Northern Ireland, providing services to meet the needs of some of the UK's most vulnerable children and young people.

Intercountry Adoption Centre (IAC)

64-66 High Street, Barnet, Hertfordshire, EN5 5SJ
Tel: 0870 516 8742
info@icacentre.org.uk
www.icacentre.org.uk
IAC aims to ensure that people contemplating adoption from another country have the means of making informed decisions, with a clear understanding of the issues involved. They also offer specialist support and help to families and young adopted people after the adoption has taken place, and help to make contact with other adoptive families.

The Post Adoption Centre (PAC)

5 Torriano Mews, Torriano Avenue, London, NW5 2RZ
Tel: 020 7284 0555
advice@postadoptioncentre.org.uk
www.postadoptioncentre.org.uk
The Post-Adoption Centre (PAC) provides counselling and therapeutic support to all parties in the adoption process – namely birth mothers, adopted children and adoptive parents – and to professionals working with them.

Tax Credits Helpline

Tel: 08453 003 900
The Tax Credits Helpline is provided by the HMRC and gives information on tax credits available, how to apply and help with claims.

For foster carers and potential foster carers

Fosterline

PO Box 51566,London, SE1 8WJ
Tel: 0800 040 7675
fosterline@fostering.net
www.fostering.net
Fosterline, part of the Fostering Network, is the confidential advice line for foster carers, providing independent, impartial advice about fostering issues. As well as providing information, Fosterline is able to advise foster carers on how to take the next step in dealing with any fostering-related problems and offers advice on how to access other services and support.

Fostering Network

87 Blackfriars Road, London, SE1 8HA
Tel:
England 020 7620 6400
Scotland 0141 204 1400
Ireland 028 9070 5056
Wales 029 2044 0940
info@fostering.net
www.fostering.net
The fostering network is focused on improving foster care and making a positive difference for children and young people in and leaving foster care. They do this by working with foster carers and fostering services. They provide information, advice, training and other forms of support for their members, and are involved in a variety of projects UK wide.

For adoptees

After Adoption

Canterbury House, 12 -14 Chapel Street, Manchester, M3 7NH
Tel: 0161 839 4932
information@afteradoption.org.uk
www.afteradoption.org.uk
After Adoption provide two national telephone helplines: ActionLine for adults (0800 0 568 578) and a unique young persons helpline, TALKadoption (0808 808 1234). Trained telephone counsellors offer advice, support and an impartial friendly ear. After Adoption provides information, support and advice to all those affected by adoption and throughout the adoption process. They have a family finding service and they work with particularly 'hard to place' young children, working towards the stability needed for a happier future.

Norcap

112 Church Road, Wheatley, Oxfordshire, 0X33 1LU
Tel: 01865 875000
enquiries@norcap.org
Norcap helps adults affected by adoption, working to reduce distress and anxiety. They do this by giving information, support and advice. Norcap operate a register to link people separated by adoption and help facilitate reunions.

Book List

Adoption

Adopting a Child: A Guide for People Interested in Adoption

By Jennifer Lord, BAAF, London, 2006, £8.50.

Considering Adoption (Overcoming Common Problems)

By Sarah Biggs, Sheldon Press, London, 2001, £6.99.

First Steps in Parenting the Child Who Hurts: Tiddlers and Toddlers

By Caroline Archer, Jessica Kingsley Publishers, London, 1999, £13.95.

The Primal Wound: Understanding the Adopted Child

By Nancy Verrier, Lafayette, USA, 1993, £9.50.

Real Parents, Real Children: Parenting the Adopted Child

By Holly Van Gulden and Lisa Bartels-Rabb, Crossroad Publishing Company, New York, USA, 1996, £11.99.

Related by Adoption: A Handbook for Grandparents and Other Relatives

By Hedi Argent, BAAF, London, 2004, £6.50.

Fostering

Fostering a Child: A Guide for People Interested in Fostering

By Henrietta Bond, BAAF, London, 2004, £8.50.

If You Don't Stick with Me, Who Will?: The Challenges and Rewards of Foster Care

By Henrietta Bond, BAAF, London, 2005, £8.95.

Providing a Secure Base in Long-term Foster Care

By Mary Beek and Gillian Schofield, BAAF, London, 2004, £13.95.

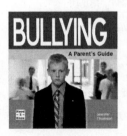